Reclaim Your Life, Reclaim Yourself

A Guide for Victims of Domestic Violence

Alison Pourteau,
M.A., LPC-Supervisor

First Kindle Edition: May 2019
Revised Edition: October 2025

Contents

Introduction to This Guidebook

The purpose of this guidebook is twofold:

1. To discuss options for dealing with domestic violence (DV) while understanding each situation is unique.
2. To help you make a reasonable exit plan if you choose to leave the relationship.

This guide is aimed at those who are in an abusive situation—or believe they may be—and the loved ones who want to help but don't know what to do. I'll do my best to provide as many resources as possible while keeping things short and to the point. (See Appendix A in this guide for a resource list.) Throughout the guide and to help illustrate how others experience abuse, I'll cite real stories from real people. I've changed the names to protect survivors' privacy.

One quick note: I considered trying to remain gender-neutral given the fact that there are male victims and victims in LGBTQ relationships. However, it's a statistical fact that most abusers are men and most victims are women, and this is reflected in my experiences working with clients. Nevertheless, I have worked with enough male victims and other non-typical victims to understand that there are many similarities, as well as differences, in the way abuse can manifest. I hope that, whatever your gender or the gender of your abuser, you'll be able to overlook any pronouns that don't match your particular situation and still gain valuable insights from this guidebook. In particular, I hope it will help you *stay safe* and *find the freedom to live your life without fear.*

My goal for these guidelines is to help you stay safe
and find the freedom to live your life without fear.

PART 1

Assessing the Relationship

I am not concerned that you have fallen—
I am concerned that you arise.
— Abraham Lincoln

What Is Abuse? Am I in an Abusive Relationship?

As a society, we tend to have a limited definition of abuse; we think of a woman with a black eye and a busted lip. But abusive relationships are much more complex than the physical violence that may, or may not, occur. Abuse is about control, and attempts for one human being to control another can come in many forms. Here are some of the examples my clients have used to describe their relationships with their abusive partners:

- "I was often the only one working. He blew through the money as soon as I got paid, but he would get upset if I wanted to get my nails done, telling me we didn't need to waste money on something like that."

- "He and my best friend got into what I thought was a friendly, even joking, debate about how the Bible says wives should submit to their husbands. He didn't seem upset by it at the time, but after that, he would get irritated any time I talked about her or wanted to hang out with her. He never came out and said I couldn't, but he would criticize her all the time and would be cold to me after I spent time with her. It got to where I didn't see her as much just because I didn't enjoy it anymore. I was too worried about what I would have to put up with when I got home."

- "I can remember feeling frustration and indignation so intense I would shake. No matter how rational my argument, I couldn't win. He was a master at twisting my words and making it all my fault."

- "I was expected to spend every free moment I had with him when he was home. If he was fixing the car, I needed to be sitting on a stool in the garage. If he was watching a show I wasn't interested in, I still had to be on the couch beside him. I couldn't even get up to go to the bathroom without him questioning where I was going!"

> As a society, we tend to have a limited definition of abuse. Abuse is about control, and attempts for one human being to control another can come in many forms.

The best resource I can recommend for providing specific examples of abuse is the Deluth Model Power and Control Wheel. I suggest taking a minute to look it over or watch the video explanation of the wheel (https://www.theduluthmodel.org/wheels/) before moving on.

Deluth Model Power and Control Wheel

Most people do not experience all the types of abuse, and there are not a specific number of "yes" answers that tell you you're experiencing abuse. I would recommend highlighting the ones you've experienced. I often find that victims don't realize how much of what they've come to assume is a normal part of daily life is actually *a form of abuse or control*.

Maggie, a client, talks about the first red flags she remembers. They appeared soon after she and Tom were married.

> He found wet clothes sitting in the washer. He asked me how long they'd been there. I told him I'd started the washer that morning but forgot to move them to the dryer.
>
> He got right in my face and started screaming at me! He said they were mildewed. He demanded that I rewash them immediately. I did, even though they seemed fine, but he kept bringing it up, saying that his clothes smelled like mildew and complaining about how bad I am at housekeeping. There really was nothing wrong with them! I even looked up how long it takes mold to grow, but that made him even more furious. He said I was always trying to start an argument and make him look stupid, that I thought I was better than him. I felt so guilty! I was pleading with him, telling him how I never meant to make him feel that way and I really did think he was intelligent. From that day on, I was *obsessive* about drying the clothes as soon as they finished in the wash."

A Word on Emotional Abuse

Most people, when they think of the word "abuse," think of a man punching, slapping, or kicking a woman, but this stereotype is so far from the common experience. Even if you assume that the victim is female, nothing else about the stereotype holds true. Most women in abusive relationships rarely, if ever, are physically attacked. Of those that are, I've had numerous women tell me basically the same thing: "The bruises will heal. It's the words I can't get out of my head."

Verbal and emotional abuse can take many forms, and an abuser is a pro at figuring out what will hurt the most. Why actually hit the person when punching the wall or throwing a glass will get them in line and not leave any marks? She'll clean up the mess, and the holes in the sheetrock will serve as a good reminder. Did she lose her first child to SIDS when the baby was only a few months old? Hiding or threatening to destroy the photo album of the only existing pictures will get her to do whatever you want. Not all bruises are on the outside. Many victims secretly beg for their abuser to hit them, to leave a visible mark that they can point to and say, "This is why I'm leaving him!" But it's not the physical pain that will haunt them, even if they do get out. It will be the words, spoken with contempt and resentment, saying, "You're worthless. There's something wrong with you. You're not good enough. No one else will want you. This is all your fault."

Who Is Most at Risk for Being Abused?

The simple answer to this question is *everyone*. Regarding race, religion, socioeconomic status (SES), etc., the only differences tend to be in the details. A victim's SES can have a huge impact on her ability to access and benefit from support services.

Income Level Matters

Income level affects a survivor's likelihood of seeking and obtaining help. For example, an abuser in a higher SES bracket may have an influential job or be seen as a pillar of the community. As a result, his wife may not receive the same level of acceptance or assistance as other victims because the community doesn't immediately recognize him as the "abusive type" (or her as a likely victim). He can afford to bribe the children or hire expensive lawyers to fight for custody. If she has a professional career, she may fear what damage he will do to her job and reputation.

> A victim's socioeconomic status can have a huge impact on her ability to access and benefit from support services.

For a woman from a lower SES bracket, the main concern may be that her abuser is the primary breadwinner. If she leaves him—and particularly if he's in jail—she can lose access to any financial support he provides. Even if she's working or able to find a job, the idea of paying bills and being able to afford daycare for their children with one minimum-wage job can seem laughably absurd.

Getting Help Is Key to Ending the Abuse

Every situation is different. Every victim will have her own obstacles to overcome, as well as her own strengths that can help her overcome them. Every assessment of each relationship—every safety plan—must be unique to the victim and the person they're considering leaving. This is why I encourage everyone in an abusive relationship—or simply in an unhealthy relationship—to talk to a professional. Get an outside opinion on what is going on to assess the health and potential risks of the relationship.

> Every assessment of each relationship—every safety plan—must be unique to the victim and the person they're considering leaving.

Finding a professional counselor or psychologist isn't a requirement. Call the **National Domestic Violence** hotline and talk with someone there about your concerns. Ask them: is what I'm experiencing abuse? There's no harm in calling a free number and getting free advice, as long as you can do so safely, without risking your partner finding out. (For example, call from someone else's phone when the abuser is not around.) At the very least, you'll be better informed and better able to move forward in making a healthy decision about your life and your relationship.

Resource: The National Domestic Violence Hotline
1-800-799-7233
www.thehotline.org
Servicios disponibles en español.

What You Deserve ... and Don't

Don't fall into the trap of believing that your experience isn't bad enough. Any form of abuse (verbal, emotional, financial, etc.), no matter how severe or how infrequent, is too much. You deserve better. You deserve basic respect. You deserve to be treated as a human being, just like any other person you or your partner would pass on the street. In fact—as the most important person in your partner's life—you should be treated with at least as much consideration as he treats friends, or even random strangers whom he happens to interact with in daily life:

> Tracy hated the way Kevin would speak so vulgarly in front of her. In particular, it upset her that he didn't seem to care if the kids were around. However, he never spoke that way in front of his parents, and his mother would never take Tracy seriously when she tried to explain what he was like.

Making the Excuse for Abuse

Tomorrow, you promise yourself, will be different, yet, tomorrow is too often a repetition of today. — James T. McKay

Anyone suffering abuse at the hands of a loved one will almost inevitably downplay what they've gone through, whether they were physically abused or not. If the abuse is primarily verbal and emotional, you will tell yourself, "Well, he's never touched me." If he slaps you, the thought will be, "It's not like he ever *punched* me." If he beats you, you make excuses about how infrequently it happens or respond with "Yeah, but I got him good, too!" Or, you make excuses for the behavior. Here are some rationalizations for suffering abuse I've heard from the D V survivors I've worked with:

- "He's having a really hard time at work. His boss is really being unfair to him and it's making him really stressed out."

- "He was so horribly abused growing up. He never had a good model of what love was. He's really trying his best."

- "Of course he's jealous after the way his exes cheated on him. I'll prove to him that I'm not like them."

> Don't fall into the trap of believing that your experience isn't bad enough. Any form of abuse, no matter how severe or how infrequent, is too much. You deserve better.

So, at what point do you stop making excuses? Whatever the current explanation is for his behavior, the only thing that really matters is that it's extremely unlikely that he's ever going to change. He's certainly unlikely to change on his own unless there are consequences to motivate him. Much like the spouse of an alcoholic, you have two basic choices: stay with him and continue enabling his behavior, or begin making decisions based on what you want and what you need from the relationship.

It's Not about You

It's in most women's nature to take responsibility for the emotional care of her family. When her kids are acting out or her relationship is on the rocks, her first thought is usually, "What am I doing wrong, and how can I fix it?" In the case of an abusive relationship, this is even more apparent. Have you ever found yourself saying:

- "When will I learn to keep my mouth shut? I should have known that would start an argument?"
- "He wouldn't get so angry if I didn't screw things up. I just need to try harder."
- "He's just trying to ... (help me be a better person, keep me safe, get me to listen, etc.)."

This is not about you not being good enough. If an interaction with your partner tends to leave you feeling bad about yourself and beating yourself up, that's a good sign this is *not* a healthy relationship.

Why Does He Act This Way?

Evil is unspectacular, and always human, and shares our bed and eats at our table. — W.H. Auden

As the power broker in the relationship, the abuser is willing to go to great lengths to hurt you in ways that you would never consider. He might march up to your place of work and embarrass you, threatening your job security. He might call you names in front of your children—or even physically assault you—to show *them* who's boss, too. But why does he do these horrible things?

Power as Entitlement

To put it simply: he feels entitled, and it's worked for him ... so far. For one thing, he feels it's his right to control any (or every) aspect of your life. His actions are geared toward maintaining the power difference, with him at the top. Just as a parent has final say in what activities their kids participate in or which friends they can hang out with, the abuser feels it's his right to make decisions for your life. He expects to have his sexual needs met and his opinions accepted without question. If you fail to accept his authority, you'll be punished in some way. He twists reality to fit his own perceptions of himself and the world so that he cannot be held accountable for his own actions. Ironically, often an abuser will perceive himself as the victim, always being hurt and wronged at the hands of others. Anything he's done wrong will, in the end, be the result of someone else's—the boss's, the police officer's, *your*—mistakes, faults, and shortcomings.

> Your abuser's sense of entitlement—his belief that his way is the right (and only) way—is not something you can fix or change in him. Nor should you put up with it. You have choices.

Amy talks about the differences she noticed in herself after leaving her husband versus when she was married:

> I was always scared to let him see any negative emotions. If I was sad or depressed, he would ask why and press me for an answer. I couldn't say that

our fighting all the time made me upset because then he would rage about how it was all my fault. If I voiced my worry about finances and wondered aloud about how we were going to pay the bills that month, he would yell at me for intentionally causing him stress. I'd try to hide when I was crying—but he was always watching me. I didn't even have the freedom of my own emotions!

I didn't realize how bad it was until after the separation. I'll be driving home and start freaking out because I wouldn't make it in the allowed 10 minutes I had to get home after work. I was going to have to hear the "you're a worthless wife and mother" lecture.

Then, I realize that I was going home to my own place, that he's not there, and I could feel my whole body start to relax. After the divorce, my chronic back pain just went away!

The Parent-Child Dynamic

As I mentioned, the abuser sees himself as your superior—as the parent to the child—which is why he demands respect but chooses not to show it to you in kind. He will manipulate you, denying and minimizing the abuse, and feel completely justified in anything he's said or done. If you hadn't done X, Y, or Z, he believes these problems wouldn't exist. And, yes, he is in control of his actions.

In the end, it comes down to this: an abuser chooses to behave the way he does because he feels he has every right to do so and it gets him what he wants:

- His food is hot and waiting for him when he walks in the door.

- His kids are being raised with minimal effort on his part.

- Money is being spent how he sees fit.

- His house is kept neat and tidy, to his specifications.

Whatever his particular needs and desires, they are being met. Why should he change?

This may be so foreign to how you think and behave that you have a hard time understanding it. You may never fully wrap your mind around that explanation, but you don't have to—you just need to accept it as a fact. Unfortunately, wishing things were different won't help your situation. In the end, the responsibility is on you to make a change for your own benefit. Educate yourself. Determine what boundaries you want to set and what the consequences of crossing them will be for him. Decide what changes you need and the safest way of bringing those changes about. His sense of entitlement—his belief that his way is the right (and only) way—is not something you can fix or change in him. Nor is it something you have to put up with. You have choices.

What If He Has Mental Illness?

I've had numerous clients that wondered if their abusive partner might suffer from mental illness because his moods would change so suddenly, without warning. They hoped that if he could just get on medication, everything would be better. However, when I asked about the abuser's behavior outside the home—such as in front of his boss or his parents—most survivors told me that he rarely, if ever, lost control publicly. He didn't scream obscenities at his boss or physically attack his parents. He only acted out in the privacy of his own home and with his immediate family.

Sufferers of mental illness rarely exhibit violence, and they certainly cannot control when and where their symptoms will occur. So, while some abusers undoubtedly have mental health conditions, those conditions—*if* they have them—are no excuse for abusive behavior and cannot be medicated away. They are two separate issues, and *both* must be addressed.

Or a Substance Abuse Problem?

Are there connections between substance abuse and intimate partner violence? Absolutely! Are abused children more likely to end up in an abusive relationship? Again, the answer is yes. Are these the reasons that your partner is abusing you?

No! It's not!

Drugs and alcohol can certainly lower an abuser's inhibitions, and if your partner does abuse substances, you should consider yourself to be at a higher risk of danger. However, there are lots of people in the world who have problems with drugs or alcohol but do not abuse others. Again, these are two separate issues, and fixing one will not fix the other. It's like assuming that taking an antibiotic for your sinus infection will cause your lower back pain to go away. Both problems may contribute to making you feel miserable, but you can't expect to target one problem and have all of them go away.

Or Was Abused as a Child?

Does witnessing or having experienced abuse as a child make someone more likely to be an abuser? Absolutely! However, having suffered abuse as a child is also not an excuse for abusive behavior in adulthood. Many people experience unhappy, even horrific, childhoods but do not go on to abuse their loved ones. No matter what we went through as children, our actions as adults are our own. Yes, our childhoods have a significant impact on our adult lives, but as adults, we have a responsibility to make different choices and to seek out help if we can't do it on our own. No one would accept the excuse from an alcoholic that they grew up in an alcoholic family so there's nothing they can do about their drinking. We would tell them to see a counselor, join AA, go to rehab, or pursue any number of other options.

Adult survivors of child abuse have the same obligations. They cannot change their past, but they can take steps to heal from it. If they aren't willing to do so, then that is their choice. If that's the choice they make, you need to accept it, not keep pushing them to change. If they are unwilling to take the steps necessary to deal with their issues, you have to focus on yourself and your own choices. Basically, you will need to decide if you want to continue living as you are and accept the relationship as it is. If you cannot, then your focus should be on what you want to change about *your* life.

Couples Counseling Is Not a Good Idea at This Point...

As someone who's worked with a number of different clients—both individually and with couples—I don't recommend couples counseling if you're in an abusive relationship. In fact, if I find out that a couple I'm working with is experiencing abuse, I no longer consider it ethical to counsel them as a couple. This is not because I think the relationship problems are all the abuser's fault. Couples counseling makes the basic assumption that both individuals have issues to work on within the relationship. The primary goal is to help them communicate better so that both people feel heard and understood by their partner.

When abuse is present, there is no solid foundation upon which to build a better relationship through improved communication between partners. It would be akin to saying, "One of you is unemployed and shooting up heroin on a daily basis, while the other person works and tries to maintain a normal household, but we're going to treat you as two people with equal responsibility for the problems in the marriage and assume that better communication will fix everything."

In addition, couples counseling can be unsafe for the victim in the relationship. In front of the counselor, the abuser may seem very contrite and agreeable to admitting his flaws. But often—behind the closed doors of the family home—a different reality exists. He's angry and resentful about what you said to the counselor and "how bad you made him look"; how much you *embarrassed him*. In the end, it often becomes impossible for the abused spouse to speak openly and honestly, which is an absolute requirement for any counseling (individual or couples) to be effective.

> When abuse is present, there is no solid foundation upon which to build a better relationship through improved communication between partners. In fact, couples counseling can be unsafe for the victim in the relationship.

Kathie describes what an argument looks like in her relationship, and why she got to the point of never expressing her own ideas or opinions:

> We could have a fight over the stupidest, most mundane things. And I don't really like arguing. In fact, I would often try to just let him win. Saying "we can both agree to disagree" didn't work because he couldn't agree to that. I had to admit that he was right.
>
> But even if I said, "Yeah, you're probably right," that wasn't the end of it. He would just keep going

on and on, repeating himself and yelling and down-grading me because I dared to contradict him. It was like I wasn't supposed to have an opinion if it was different from his in any way.

> Whether you want to come to terms with the problems in the relationship or just want to focus on yourself, therapy can help.

...But Individual Counseling Can Save Your Life

As much as I recommend against couples counseling, finding a therapist who can work with you individually is a must. A therapist can help you gain perspective, determine if what you are experiencing is abuse, and help outline what your options are. However, they will not tell you what to do. Whether you want to come to terms with the problems in the relationship or just want to focus on yourself, therapy can help.

For example, many victims of domestic violence suffer from depression or anxiety. To cope, some turn to drugs or alcohol or food—anything to distract them from or anesthetize them against the pain of being hurt by the one who supposedly loves them most. They might find themselves so stressed out they become short tempered or yell at their kids. Whatever it is you're dealing with, individual therapy can help.

Just as in any profession, some therapists are better than others. Or, you might simply not have a good fit with the first therapist you talk to. *Keep trying.* Having the support of a professional—particularly one that understands domestic violence—can prove vital, not only to helping you get out of an abusive relationship, but to your long-term recovery as well. And there are many agencies out there that will provide counseling services free of charge, whether you are still in the relationship or not. Contact your local DV agency, 211, or the National Domestic Violence Hotline to find resources in your area. (See the "Resources" section of this guidebook.)

Do It for the Children …
But Does That Mean *Stay* or *Go*?

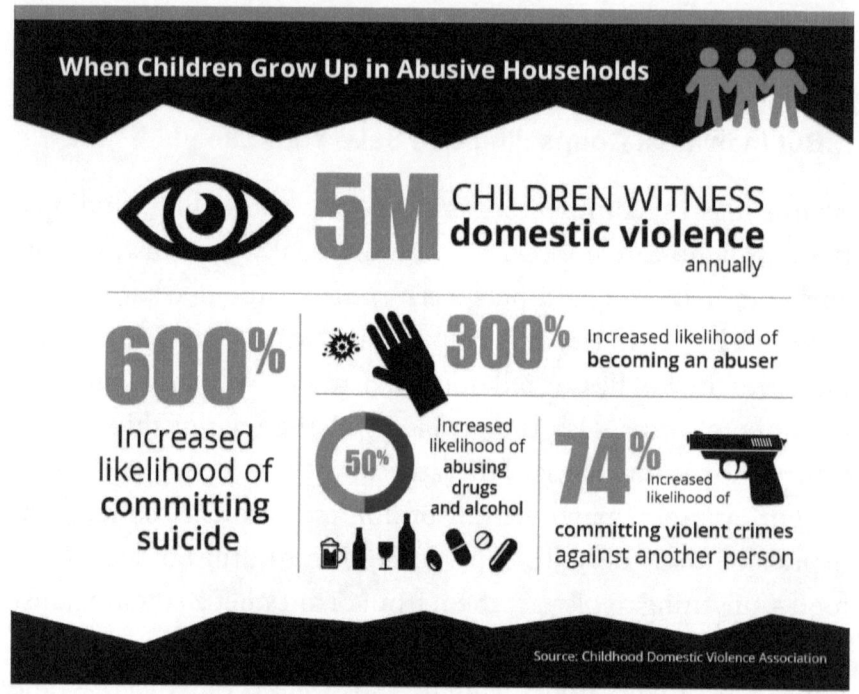

When Children Grow Up in Abusive Households

5M CHILDREN WITNESS **domestic violence** annually

600% Increased likelihood of **committing suicide**

300% Increased likelihood of **becoming an abuser**

50% Increased likelihood of **abusing drugs and alcohol**

74% Increased likelihood of **committing violent crimes against another person**

Source: Childhood Domestic Violence Association

Happy families are all alike. Every unhappy family is unhappy in its own way. — Leo Tolstoy

As I keep saying, every relationship is different, and this is especially so when it comes to deciding what is best for your children. One of the first questions I'd like you to consider is: how would you feel about your children growing up and having a relationship just like yours? Would you be okay with your child marrying a spouse like yours? Or, are you horrified at the idea? Maybe you wish for them to find a partner more supportive of them.

Answering these questions will help determine how important it is, for the children's sake, that you leave the abuser. Remember, your children learn by observing their parents, and that includes how to treat other people. Not every child that grows up seeing abuse becomes involved in an abusive relationship, but it is does put them at much greater risk for either becoming an abuser or becoming a victim. According to the Childhood Domestic Violence Association, children who grow up in a household where domestic violence exists often suffer from post-traumatic stress disorder; the effects on their brain are similar to those experienced by combat veterans.

Resource: The Childhood Domestic Violence
Association
1-212-330-8016
https://cdv.org/

You Are the Expert Here

Though there is never one right answer for all situations, staying together for the children is *not* in their best interests, in most cases. Some women stay because they fear their children being harmed if they are not there to prevent it, such as when the children have unsupervised visitation with their father. Some women, in choosing to leave, have had to leave their children behind. Or the abuser might have gained full custody following a divorce and the victim only has visitation. More often than not, I find that abusers aren't interested in the full-time responsibilities of being a single parent, but you have to assess your own situation.

The most qualified expert on how much risk the children will be in if you leave is *you*—the mother who's considering leaving.

Staying for the children might be necessary to keep them physically safe. However, there is little you can do to protect them emotionally while remaining in the abusive environment. Even if you think that the abuser is a good father and would never physically hurt the children, they're already being hurt by the environment they're living in.

In an Abusive Home, There Are No Secrets

No matter how well you think you are hiding it from them—maybe you argue with your husband behind a closed bedroom door—you can't hide the way their father treats you in front of them. You can't hide your fear of his moods and emotions, which can be expressed, for example, in body language your children see. Children are like sponges. They soak up the emotions in their surroundings. They may choose not to hear you when you say it's bedtime, but they'll absolutely hear the anger and contempt in his words. Abuse becomes normalized when children see it every day, and because it seems the normal thing to do, they're much more likely to treat others that way—or put up with being treated that way—both in childhood and later in their adult life.

Another tragic aspect of children and domestic violence—*they often blame themselves for the abuse they witness*. Children tend to see the world in very black-and-white terms. If bad things are happening, it's because someone deserves it. Children often assume it's their having done something wrong—being bad—that makes Daddy mad and hit Mommy. If they turn the blame inward for the violence they see, they can strive to be perfect and make everyone else happy. (This is how a child from an abusive situation can become the victim later in life in their own adult relationship.) If they turn the blame outward, they can become angry and aggressive, taking out their internal pain on anyone they feel has wronged them, including you. (This is how a child can become an abuser.)

What's Important in Making the Decision to Leave

Choosing to stay in a relationship so that your children don't have to leave their home or lose their "intact" family is like choosing to stay in a war zone because you don't want to give up your nice house. Though you can't always protect your children from what's going on around them, you can teach them how to handle difficult situations. You can be a role model for them about how a woman, or any person, deserves to be treated—and how they can become their own champion if they're not treated with respect.

I'm not saying that it's easy, for you or the children, but it's important to accept that you can't protect them from all harm. Your job is to prepare them to survive in the real world, a world that is not always fair and is sometimes painful. It's your job to teach them how to stand up for themselves while still being caring to others. You're responsible for showing them how to overcome obstacles and never give up.

> You can be a role model for them about how a woman, or any person, deserves to be treated—and how they can become their own champion if they're not treated with respect.

No child requires two parents, a picket fence, and a dog to have a happy life—but he or she does need to know what it means to feel safe. Children need to be able to trust that the people around them will be there for them and protect them.

Pets (Our Other Children)

For many victims who are fortunate enough not to have to worry about sharing a child with the abuser, there is still another concern that weighs almost as heavily on their hearts: their pets. There is a very strong link between domestic violence and animal abuse, and as with children, an abuser is more than happy to exploit a beloved pet in the same way that he would exploit a child. Often, the abuse of the pet occurs in front of the mother and children. Not only does this help create an environment of fear, it can serve to keep the humans in the home submissive. After all, if the abuser gets angry, he might take it out on a defenseless pet. The only way to prevent this is to try to keep him happy.

An abuser will also use pets to keep a victim from leaving or convince her to return. I have known many women who would not consider entering a shelter because they could not bring their pets with them. However, just like children, animals are not safe in such an environment. Reach out to family or friends who might be willing to take care of your pet if you have to leave. Call the local animal shelter or animal fostering program. Many will house pets, on a temporary basis, until the victim is ready to reclaim them. Or, visit the Animal Welfare Institute's Safe Havens Mapping Project to find a sheltering service near you.

Resource: Animal Welfare Institute's
Safe Havens Mapping Project
https://awionline.org/safe-havens

Odds Are, He's Not Going to Change—So You Have To

> *As I grow older, I pay less attention to what men say.*
> *I just watch what they do. — Andrew Carnegie*

Numbers to Know

Up to 83 percent of women entering DV shelters reported their partners also abused or killed the family pet.[1]

Up to 48 percent of DV victims delay leaving a dangerous situation because of concerns regarding their pets' welfare.[2]

1 The Humane Society of the United States

2 Mayor's Alliance for NYC's Animals

It's likely you still hold onto hope for a better future, and that future is absolutely possible—but likely not in the way you've been dreaming about. Your partner is probably not going to (*finally!*) be financially stable or stop drinking or realize how much the kids need him and become the person you thought he was when you fell in love. You might see glimpses of that person on occasion. It's what keeps you in the relationship when you're so angry and frustrated. Those glimmers of hope keep us going, keep us believing that it would be wrong to give up, that you'd be quitting too soon, that there's still a chance that *this time*, things will be different. But how many *this times* have there been?

A friend told me a story that I think perfectly describes this situation:

> You wake up and realize you're in a bucket of shit, up to your mouth and you are on your toes. You can see the ladder to get out, but when you start to move, it stirs up the shit and the flies go everywhere and some gets in your hair and mouth and it sucks really bad. So, you get still again. Then, you start to rationalize being there. "At least it's warm, and nothing can get me here." So, you

stay in the shit because starting to move is so miserable and uncomfortable.

It's natural to make excuses for the people we love, to protect other people's image of them just as we want to protect the person himself. But keep in mind, we're not talking about a child who commits thoughtless acts; we're talking about an adult making the conscious decision to abuse you.

Try this mind exercise. Imagine the things your husband or boyfriend has said and done to you throughout your relationship. Now, imagine yourself treating your child, or even a friend, that way. If they talked back, would you feel justified in slapping them? If they had a different opinion on something, would you scream in their face and tell them how stupid they are? If you cannot justify doing these things—even to someone who has behaved badly—then why make excuses for someone who treats you this way? You *are* an adult. You have a right to make your own choices and decisions about how to live your life, free from fear, ridicule, or blame, and the right to be treated with basic respect.

Adults are accountable for their own decisions and actions. If those actions are working for them, why would they change? Every abuser has his own priorities and issues over which he wants control. For some, they want the house clean and a hot meal ready when they walk in the door. Others want to control whom you talk to, whether you're allowed to have friends, or how often you can visit your family. Some want you bringing in a steady income and paying all the bills.

Whatever it is they expect, whatever apologies they may offer for their abusive behavior, keeping you under their control provides them what they want. You're someone who takes care of their needs, be it a babysitter for the kids or someone to be with them, constantly at their side.

Give up the dream that your abuser will change.

Is it possible? Sure.

Is it likely? No.

They have no reason to change because there are no real consequences to their abusive behavior. If you want your life to change, to get better, then you have to make change happen for yourself.

Adults are accountable for their own decisions and actions. Give up the dream that your abuser will change. Make change happen for yourself.

PART 2

Leaving Your Abuser

You gain strength, courage and confidence by every experience in which you really stop to look fear in the face. You are able to say to yourself, "I have lived through this horror. I can take the next thing that comes along." You must do the thing you think you cannot do.
— *Eleanor Roosevelt*

Throw Out the "How to Break Up with Your Boyfriend" Handbook

Safety is the first and most important thing to think about if you're considering leaving an abusive relationship. As I talk about safety planning and how to leave your abuser, you might think, "He would never _____." Fill in the blank with your choice. He would never…

- Get physical?
- Use the children?
- Kill your pet?
- Try to turn your family and friends against you?

He's No Longer the Man You Fell in Love With

When you were dating and falling in love with him, did you ever think he'd ever talk to you the way he does now? Did you ever imagine you'd be afraid of him? Did you dream you'd be constantly walking on eggshells trying to keep him happy? Did you think there'd ever be a day when—if you tried to talk to him about how unhappy you are—instead of sympathy, you'd receive ridicule or blame, or (if you were lucky) he'd simply ignore you? You might not have known back then what he was capable of or what he'd turn into, so don't assume you know how he'll react now when he learns you're leaving him.

> Safety is the first and most important thing to think about if you're considering leaving an abusive relationship.

One of the most important safety precautions you can take is to *avoid sitting down face to face alone with him in your home* to have the "I just can't do this anymore" talk. Remember, this man has systematically abused you; he's driven you to the point of wanting to leave. He isn't someone you can expect to sit and listen calmly to your concerns. If he cared about your feelings, he wouldn't be abusing you in the first place. He isn't likely to let you simply walk out the door. It's much more likely he'll try to prevent you—even physically—from leaving. He'll take your car keys, destroy your phone, threaten to hurt you, himself, or the kids—whatever it takes to keep you there, in that house, under his control.

Remember, you don't have to leave immediately. Not every situation is bad enough that you need to sneak out in the middle of the night, change your name, and move across the country. However, be aware that whatever he's done or threatened to do before, you can expect him to take it farther—to become more dramatic, more controlling, more physically threatening—once he knows you're intent on leaving. No matter how obvious it's been to you that the relationship isn't working, he might be completely oblivious. After all, it's been working for *him*. Your announcement that you wish to leave could very well come as a complete shock to him. Often men who don't know how to handle emotional situations in a healthy way will fall back on the one emotion they are most comfortable with: *anger*. You've already been his target. Imagine how he might react now that he knows *you*, his prized possession, are about to leave him.

His Perspective: You're His, and Possessions Don't Leave

The idea that you're his possession might surprise you. Or, it might not. But in many ways, your abuser considers you to be his possession, much like his home or his car. He can treat his car however he wants. He can drive too fast over potholes and fill the inside with trash if he so chooses. It doesn't matter what he does to the car, good or bad; it's his, and he expects it to be there, sitting in his driveway, when he wants to use it. If he walks outside one day and finds his car is gone, how do you think he will respond? Would telling him, "Well, you never did take good care of it" make any difference in his response or lessen his anger?

Resource: Mosaic Threat Assessment Systems
https://www.mosaicmethod.com/
Remember: access Mosaic from a safe computer—located, for example, in a public library or at a friend's house—and using an email address your abuser cannot access or monitor.

Just as he would prevent a car thief from stealing his car, expect the same when it comes to you leaving—even if *you're the thief* trying to "steal you" from him. If you haven't had control over your choices and actions during the relationship, why would he allow you to take that control from him now? In his mind, *you're his*. And the idea that you would decide to leave him will likely infuriate him. Expect his abusive behaviors to get louder, more manipulative, and even more physically violent. Those strategies have worked for him in the past, and as he perceives his world crumbling around him—as the reality of your leaving sets in—he'll dial those strategies up to 11.

But, as I've said before, everyone's situation is unique. To assess the risk you might face in leaving the relationship, start with Gavin de Becker's website Mosaic at https://www.mosaicmethod.com/. *Make sure that you are using a safe computer*, such as at a library or a friend's house—somewhere, in other words, where he won't know what you're doing—before taking this assessment. Once on the website, click on the type of situation you're currently facing.

You will need to register on Mosaic before you can take the assessment, so use an email address that your abuser can't access.

Even if you find that you are not in the high-risk category, go over the safety precautions listed below and implement as many as possible. Just like every Californian should have an earthquake kit and every Kansan a basement to shelter in, it never hurts to be too cautious. In fact, when it comes to ensuring your safety when leaving an abuser, there's no such thing as too cautious.

When it comes to ensuring your safety when leaving an abuser, there's no such thing as too cautious.

What If I'm Not Ready to Give up Completely?

Love never dies a natural death. It dies because we don't know how to replenish its source. It dies of blindness and errors and betrayals. It dies of illness and wounds; it dies of weariness, of witherings, of tarnishings. — Anaïs Nin

I always recommend to women that even if they are not ready to give up on the relationship completely, they consider at least a one-year separation. That may seem like a long time, but I'd guess that you've been unhappy and putting up with abuse much longer than that. If your spouse really wants to work things out, a year is not a long time. Significant changes need to happen in not only his behavior but in his thinking process.

Your responsibility during the separation is to focus on taking care of yourself and your children and maintaining boundaries with your spouse. If you've made it clear that he's not welcome to show up at your home uninvited, don't open the door to him when you see him on the doorstep. If at some point in the separation period you *both* agree to start dating again, stick to the one day a week you've agreed upon for date night. Don't be coerced or pressured into seeing him more often or having daily phone conversations (or any other contact). If he is really going to change—again, an extremely unlikely event—then his accepting and respecting your boundaries have to be the first step in demonstrating his commitment to making that change. If you set boundaries and he becomes angry, manipulative, or resentful and reverts back to his abusive behavior, then you have a better idea of how committed to changing he really is (or isn't).

Not ready to give up yet? Establish a trial period for separation. Test his willingness to accept your boundaries. His response will show you just how committed he is (or isn't) to changing.

Safety Planning 101

A woman must not depend on the protection of man, but must be taught to protect herself. — *Susan B. Anthony*

What Do You Mean, Honey? Everything's Great! Let Me...

...fill in the blank with what you know will calm him down.

Abusers usually become very suspicious, even paranoid, when they feel you're pulling away or they're not able to control you to the same extent they used to. As much as you might try to act as if everything is business as usual, simply being more apathetic to their verbal abuse can make them suspicious and begin upping the stakes. Your body language and tone of voice—unconsciously and unintentionally—can tip off observant abusers. So be careful in personal interactions to seem business as usual, even while planning your escape.

Be nice to him. Make plans for the future. Take care of him, as you always have—make his dinner, nurse him when he's sick, whatever you've done in the past to placate him. It will likely be necessary to continue having sex with him—do whatever it takes to keep yourself safe. There's light at the end of the tunnel, and planning is the first step in moving toward it.

This advice might seem manipulative, but would you fault a kidnapping victim for lying to their captor or "playing nice" in order to increase their chance of escaping safely? Your situation is no different. You know that he's capable of hurting you emotionally and maybe physically. He created this situation. The only obligation you have is to yourself and, if you have children, to your kids—do whatever you need to get out safely.

Packing an Emergency (Get-Away) Bag

Even if you do your best to act normally and keep things as calm as possible, your need to leave might prove immediate. I recommend having an emergency (get-away) bag packed and stored in a safe place at all times. That could be at a friend's house, your office, or even hidden in the trunk of your car. Just *be sure that it's not a place where he's likely to find it* and question you about why it's there. Finding your get-away bag might itself be a trigger to violence for him. Your number-one priority is to be safe—in all planning, preparation, and execution of your departure strategy.

What to Pack in Your GetAway Bag

- Medication
- Spare keys (house, car, work, etc.)
- Money
- Extra clothes for you and your kids
- Calling cards or cheap burner phone
- Baby's needs (things you'd pack in a diaper bag)
- Children's favorite stuffed animals, blankets, etc.
- Important documents (photocopied or original)
- Sentimental/valuable items (photo album or jewelry)
- List of contacts/resources

Making a Long-Term Plan to Leave

While for safety's sake you should always be prepared to leave at a moment's notice, you might have the luxury of time to more carefully and thoroughly plan your future life without your abuser in the picture.

Your goal might be to move out in six months. If everything works out and you follow through on your plan, great! If things escalate one night and you find yourself in a DV shelter or sleeping on a friend's couch, then you will at least be better prepared to pursue the life you want for yourself (and your kids) than if you hadn't started making your escape plan.

Keep in mind, you don't have to firmly commit to leaving the relationship to start planning your potential exit. Having options is always a good idea. If your partner finally decides to get treatment for his drug or alcohol use or starts seeing a counselor or makes some other move toward positive change and you decide to give him more time, that's okay too. Most people who have a fire exit strategy to flee their homes in the event of a fire hope to never use it, but that doesn't mean everyone shouldn't have a safety plan *just in case of fire*. The same is true of your safety planning for leaving your dangerous relationship.

Resource: Four Web Resources for Safety Planning

https://www.loveisrespect.org/personal-safety/create-a-safety-plan/

https://www.dvrc-or.org/safety-planning/

http://www.thehotline.org/help/path-to-safety/

https://lcadv.org/get-help/safety-planning-steps/

So, what are some of the things you can do to prepare for leaving? There are lots of great websites that offer different variations of safety plans. I suggest you look over all the ideas and figure out which ones best fit your scenario. The first thing I would suggest is opening your own checking account at a bank your partner doesn't know about and start putting away as much money as you can. It could be only $5 or $10 at a time. It's a start. If you can't do that, at least start working on a small stash of cash you can hide somewhere safe, like in your emergency get-away bag or with a friend or family member.

Strategies to Secure Your Freedom

Change any passwords he might use to access your personal plans or information—like computer, phone, and social media passwords. If you think this will be too suspicious to do while you are living with the person, be prepared to do these things as soon as you leave. *Do not keep a diary or journal* in which you talk about leaving or any of your plans.

Get a secret cell phone. One of the first things abusers will do in a bad fight, or if they think you're leaving, is to break your phone. Consider getting a new phone and keep it hidden, even if it's just a cheap burner phone.

Make a spare set of car keys. Hiding your car keys from you is a very effective way for your abuser to keep you on the premises, especially if you live in a rural area, far from potential help.

Make a spare set of house keys. I've had numerous clients locked out of their own house in the middle of the night or unable to return to get their belongings unless the abuser was home—always a potentially dangerous situation.

Decide where you'll end up, and plan for getting there. Will you want to stay in the same area or move away? If you have a job you like, family nearby, or schools you don't want to remove your kids from, begin looking for housing possibilities in your area. Figure out what you can afford, preferably without taking child support into account (since you may not be able to count on him for that either). If you don't have a job or you live in the small town where your spouse grew up and everyone knows him, you might decide that getting completely away is the best option. Realistically speaking, the fewer ties you have with your abuser—through friends, family, shared bills, etc.—and the more distance you put between you, the better odds you have of staying free of him and out of danger.

Do you have family in another city or state that would take you in, or at least be a source of emotional support? Going to a DV shelter might be the best option if you want to move far out of your abuser's reach. I've known women who were transferred to a shelter in another town because it was considered too risky for them to stay in the town where they'd been living. Some survivors pick a town, sometimes at random, and move across the country to stay in a shelter where they feel fairly certain their abuser can't find them.

Beware of spyware. Want to see something scary? Google "track my girlfriend" and see all the sites that come up—everything from YouTube videos teaching you "how to track your girlfriend's location without touching her phone" to "Top 3 Girlfriend Phone Tracker Apps."

A Basic Safety Plan

- Keep important numbers on hand (but hidden from him).
- Figure out what parts of your home are safest (easy exits and no weapons nearby).
- Think about who you could stay with if you needed to leave your home.
- Take pictures of any injuries and text/email them to someone else to keep for you.
- Establish a code word you can say to someone so he or she knows to call the police for help.
- Have a secret cell phone (even if you can only use it to call 911).
- Teach your kids to call 911.
- Open your own bank account or get a credit card in your name only.

If you are in an abusive relationship, even if your partner doesn't suspect that you are considering leaving, there's a good chance you've got spyware on your electronic devices. It's certainly more likely if he's tech savvy, but there are still plenty of "stalking tips for dummies" sites that will assist the less technologically advanced. So, how will you know if you've got spyware on your phone or computer? You may not. That's the problem, but here are some signs to look for:

- He knows exactly where you are and where you've been, when you haven't told him.

- He knows what you've looked up online, even if you deleted your history.

- He knows about conversations you've had with others, through email, text, or social media.

- Your computer is running noticeably slower.

- The battery in your cell phone drains quickly, or data usage spikes.
- Your cell phone takes a long time to shut down.

If you're not sure whether your electronics have spyware, assume they do. Don't use them for calls, texts, emails, online searches, or anything else you don't want your partner knowing about. Instead, buy a cheap burner phone, borrow a friend's, or use a library computer—anything your partner won't have access to.

If you know you have spyware, the best thing to do is to get a new phone or computer. However, that's obviously not an option for everyone. The next best thing is to do a factory reset. Write down any phone numbers and emails you want to keep. Save your pictures somewhere else or email them to someone. Then, factory reset your phone and type in all the info you want to keep. Do *not* download it from the cloud. You'll just reinstall the spyware.

Okay, I've Just Left. What Do I Do Now?

Avoid contact of any kind with the abuser. This is the most important piece of advice I can offer at this stage—and it's often the hardest for survivors to follow.

Most likely, he will try obsessively to contact you. Expect him to blow up your phone with calls, texts, and voicemails. Expect him to send emails and show up at your job. Here's what you can do:

- Don't read his texts.
- Don't answer his calls.
- Don't answer his emails.
- Don't answer the door if he knocks.

- Tell family and friends you don't want to receive messages from him. (He will use them as intermediaries to try and get to you.)

- Emphasize to other employees at your workplace that you don't want to accept calls from him and that he's not allowed to speak with you. It might even be against company policy for your workplace to acknowledge you work there at all (or are in the office at any given time); know the policies of your employer and use them to protect yourself. It's very easy for a business to enact a no-trespassing order on any individual they choose. Although it might be embarrassing to bring your personal problems to work, the highest priority is your safety.

If you keep your current phone number… Don't be surprised when you receive dozens of calls in the span of an hour. The amount and frequency of calls represent his desperation to reestablish control over your life.

Block his number, at least temporarily, but don't expect this to stop his attempts to contact you. Even though you've blocked his number, some providers will still allow him to leave voicemails; or he'll call you from another number you don't recognize, hoping you'll answer. These days, spoofing apps can make it look like your mom is calling (or mimic some other number you recognize and are more likely to answer). Let the call go to voicemail and then screen who left the message. If it's someone you want to talk to, you can call them back. Screen all your calls, especially the ones you don't recognize. Don't be surprised if he leaves desperate messages—the dog just got run over; his mother has been in a traffic accident. Most likely, these are manipulative attempts to engage with you and aren't based in reality.

You've Left. Now What?

- Don't communicate with him.
- Choose carefully with whom to share info.
- Keep any communications from him digitally.
- Expect his attempts to be more desperate.
- Seek professional (counseling) support.

Even better, get a new phone number. As I suggested earlier, get a temporary (burner) phone with a new number and *don't share the number with him.* Just as importantly—don't share it with anyone who might give it to him, either. This can include family and friends who might be sympathetic to his pleas and feel sorry for him, so they give him the number; but it can also mean family and friends entirely in your corner whom he manipulates into giving him the number (e.g., "I want to meet with her to give her money"). So, if you get a new phone number, keep to a minimum those who know it. Every single one of them—no matter how close to you and well-meaning they are—is a potential leak to your abuser.

You don't even have to hear his voice. If the temptation to listen to his messages is too great, let someone you trust listen to them and tell you if there is any important information that they feel you need to know. Pick someone who can be rational and understands the situation, not someone who is going to be easily swayed by emotions or threats or encourage you to consider his requests or to listen to his apologies. Here's one client's experience:

> Amy was describing just how charming and manipulative her husband could be. She was checking the answering machine at her office one morning and heard a message from a corrections

officer at the county jail, where her husband was being held for violating her protective order. The officer relayed the information that her husband wanted to talk to her, but it was "just about their children."

Given that Amy had had to suspend service of her home phone because her abuser would talk loudly into the answering machine, yelling for the kids and telling them to "ask Mommy why she had the bad people take me away," Amy was pretty sure he wasn't genuinely concerned about the kids' welfare. Amy described feeling a sense of hopelessness that she would ever be able to escape him completely but also a little vindicated. After all, if he could manipulate a corrections officer, of course she had been susceptible to his charm.

Keep the messages! You might have the impulse to delete his messages out of hand. Don't. The content of his messages—their harassment, threats, manipulation, etc.—can become evidence in court. You don't have to listen to them or read them, but don't throw them away. Store them digitally on a safe computer hard drive somewhere or on the cloud. Be especially careful with voice-mail messages—eventually, your voicemail box will fill up, and your provider will start auto-deleting your old messages. If you want to save those for court later, find a way to record them to a permanent storage location somewhere. For example, you could play a message via speakerphone and use your computer's built-in mic to record it to a sound file that you then store on the computer. If you don't want to hear that message yourself, have a friend do it for you. *But keep those messages!*

It's still all about power. Obviously, not every situation is the same, but I often see a pattern in how abusers behave toward their victims after separation that reminds me of the power and control wheel. Immediately after you leave, the pieces of the pie will contain such headings as *Anger*, *Regret*, *Blackmail*, and *Guilt*. You are likely to hear things like:

- "You promised you would always be there for me."
- "I'm so sorry. I'll do anything! Please, let's go to couples counseling"
- "I can't believe you would take my kids away from me!"
- "I'm going to make you pay, bitch. You're going to regret this."

In his attempts to communicate with you, the abuser will jump from topic to topic, trying one tactic after another to manipulate you into returning. If anger and accusations about your unfaithfulness fail to move you to contact him, you might get tears and sadness and promises to change. He might threaten to:

- Tell your job that you've been stealing from them.
- Post your deepest secrets on social media.
- Tell your kids that you never wanted them.
- Call your family and say that you're on drugs.
- Put in a false CPS report, claiming you're being abusive or neglectful.
- Say anything he thinks will prompt you to communicate with him, if only to beg him to stop.

It doesn't matter if what he is saying is true or not. What matters is the threat that the people in your support system will believe the stories and turn against you. He'll do whatever it takes to reestablish contact.

But what if he hurts himself? Another common tactic is the threat of self-harm. Over the course of the relationship, you might have heard how your partner "cannot live without you" or what he would do if he "ever lost you." You may be honestly concerned about him committing suicide. Although, statistically speaking, that's unlikely, even if it were to happen, *you would not be to blame.*

You cannot bind your life to another person because they threaten to harm themselves. If your abuser really is suicidal and is in fear of losing you, there is a much higher risk that he will take you with him before committing suicide if he has the opportunity. *Don't give him that opportunity.*

If you feel that you must do something to intervene, call the police and ask them to do a wellness check on him. They will send a police officer to assess his physical well-being and potential for self-harm. They also have the ability to get him professional help, which you do not.

Who will be on *my* side? In all honesty, it's very possible that people you once considered friends will side with him, or at least minimize what he did. It's human nature to avoid conflict or to believe the best about people we know and care about. Some people, believing he's basically a good guy who just needs some help, might even make excuses for him. Many people will still try to be friends with both of you. For your own safety, this just isn't an option. (Remember my warning about whom to share your new phone number with?)

You might feel betrayed and abandoned by your friends who choose to side with your abuser, but you might also find that some people in your life will stand beside you no matter what. Sometimes it's even the people you least expected to do so. If your abuser kept you so isolated that you feel you really don't have anyone in your life besides his family and friends, this is one more reason to reach out to a DV agency. Besides having advocates and counselors to help you through the process of leaving your abuser, many agencies organize support groups where you can meet other women who have been through a similar experience and know how it feels. Online groups through most social media outlets, such as Facebook, can also be helpful and supportive.

What Should I Expect from Him over the Long Term?

We've looked at what to expect from your abuser right after you've left. Now, let's look at the longer term. Over a period of weeks and months, I've observed that abusers exhibit surprisingly common patterns of behavior. Many abusers immediately begin stalking and harassing their victims. They're trying to win back the victim through, ironically, intimidation, blackmail, guilt, promises to change, etc. Sometimes that works; sometimes it doesn't. When it doesn't work, there are usually three possible behaviors exhibited by abusers:

1. **The abuser accepts that a permanent separation is going to occur**. He continues to be hateful and goes out of his way to make your life difficult, but his behavior is essentially equivalent to what you'd see in any nasty divorce: childish and petulant but usually harmless.
2. **The abuser escalates his attempts to regain power over his victim**. He is so enraged that you had the audacity to leave him and is so desperate to get you back—or at least punish you for leaving—that he ups the ante. His

attempts take physical form: he might stalk you, break into your home, damage your vehicle, etc. Besides focusing on your safety plan, work with the police as much as possible. *Get as much on the record with the police as you can so that you begin building a case against your abuser, should things escalate further.* It can be frustrating when not enough proof exists or not enough has happened to charge him. Make a report anyway; start the paper trail that could, ultimately, lead to his criminal conviction. Seek a protective order if you feel your life or the lives of your children might be in danger. If you don't feel that you are getting the support you deserve from local law enforcement, talk with the DV agency closest to you (hopefully in your community) and ask them to advocate on your behalf. You can also seek help from your victim advocates employed by local law enforcement or county and district courts.

3. **The abuser becomes distraught, promises to change, and begins to behave differently.** Often, women who still want the relationship to work will see the changes their men are making and begin the process of rebuilding the relationship. You start going out on dates again together. He offers to help out around the house and wants to spend quality time with the kids. (This newfound desire to do everything "as a family" is often just an excuse to spend more time with you.) Meanwhile, he might continue to pressure you to come back home so the two of you can "*really* work on the marriage." After a few weeks or even months, you might move back home, and for a while, things are great—until they're not. When he's comfortable that you're back, his old behaviors can reassert themselves. If he was getting counseling, look for him to come up with an excuse why he

can't continue (it might even sound logical). In the end, you can end up back where you started or worse. For example, if your family helped you move out and then watched you go right back to him (shaking their heads the whole time), they could be less willing to help you again in the future. Now that he knows you're capable of leaving him, he might hold on even tighter—making his control over you even more rigid—or he may pay little heed to threats of a separation since he's seen you come back once before.

Life for the Long Term

- Watch how he behaves. Is he really capable of change?
- Set boundaries (including for yourself). Stick to them.
- Find and use available resources (police and domestic violence advocates).
- Be aware that if you go back, leaving again could be even harder.

I don't mean to imply that change for abusers is impossible. But for real change to happen on the part of the abuser, it has to be proven over the long term and something he decides to do because it's the right thing—whether you agree to come back to him or not. Like an addict trying to get clean, he won't succeed if he's effecting change for someone else.

Take Freedom for a Test Drive

Proving his long-term intentions—and whether he's genuinely willing to (and capable of) change—is why trial separations are so important. Commit to maintaining the separation for one year. Put stopgaps into place that will help you stay strong in that commitment even when you don't feel strong: put in writing what you need him to do or change, including respecting the time limit you have set; sign a lease that's difficult to break.

If you don't feel you're ready to commit to being separated for 365 days, then you may not be ready to take the step to separate at all. That's okay. Maybe you can get away for a few days on your own, or encourage him to have a weekend with friends fishing or hunting or doing some other activity that lets you have some alone time in your home. Find a counselor to talk to, or dial up a DV hotline and speak with their on-call experts. There are lots of free services out there, and you're not required to leave your relationship to take advantage of them.

Just remember, no one but you can determine when the right time for a change is. But by the same token, once you decide change is necessary, it's up to you to make it happen.

PART 3

Now That You're Out

We must let go of the life we have planned,
so as to accept the one that is waiting for us. — Joseph Campbell

I've already discussed how to safely leave the abusive relationship. Now, let's talk about what you can do to stay safe *after* you're gone.

Secrecy for Safety

If you're able to move to a new location, do whatever you can to keep that information from your abuser. This might require limiting whom you share this information with and coaching your children on how to respond if their father questions them.

Ask any companies with which you do business—cell phone, utility, cable, etc.—to note on your account that you're the *only one allowed to get information or cancel services.* You might be embarrassed to tell them why: this is a safety issue and that you're in a DV situation. You must set aside your embarrassment to ensure your own safety (and possibly your children's safety). Disclosing the danger to them will help ensure they are more careful and take the matter of your safety seriously. (I can't tell you how many abusers make their wife's or girlfriend's life hell by canceling phone services, adding tracking information to the account, having important documents mailed to their own home instead of the woman's new address, etc.)

The Keeping Your Distance Checklist

Here's a list of precautions you can take to help maintain your safety once you're out of the relationship. The number-one, overarching safety strategy is to avoid your old habits—make new ones for your new life!

- **Get a protective order.** Provide a copy to your job, along with a picture of your ex.

- **If you are living in the same house you once shared with your abuser, change the locks as soon as possible.** Also, consider buying motion-sensor lights. Pretend your house has been targeted by thieves and outfit it to deter them.

- **If you've moved, consider getting a post office box so you don't have to give out your home address to receive bills.** This will also allow you to have your mail forwarded so that it does not end up in your ex's possession.

- **Vary your routes to work, school, home, etc., on a regular basis.** If you feel you're being followed, drive to a police station.

- **Don't shop at the same stores you used to.** It's worth the longer drive for gas or groceries in order to prevent running into your ex. And if you always shopped on Saturdays when you lived with him, pick another day of the week.

- **Open your own bank account and close any joint bank or credit card accounts.** Many banks will not let you simply take your name off an account but will let you close an account, which means both you and your ex are free to open new accounts in your own names.

- **Explain to your friends and neighbors that he is no longer living with you.** Instruct them to call you or to call the police if they see him on your street or near your house.

The number-one safety strategy is to avoid your old routines. Shop at new stores, take new routes to work, etc. Strip him of the power he had over you yesterday by making him ignorant of how you live your life *today*.

The Keeping Your Kids Safe Checklist

If you have children, there are specific things to think about when trying to keep your children safe. Here are a few of the most important considerations when safety planning with kids:

- **Practice fire drills or an emergency escape plan.** Fire drills are something kids are used to from school, though we often aren't as cautious about being prepared at home. If kids know what to do and where to go in case of a fire, they'll be more prepared for what to do in case of any other type of emergency.

- **Have a safety word.** Most abductions are committed by people the child knows, not strangers. Make sure the kids know that anyone—even family and friends—are not allowed to pick them up or take them anywhere unless they know the safety word.

- **Make your kids memorize your phone number and teach them to call you in the event your abuser takes them without permission.** Don't let them rely on knowing what Mommy's contact photo looks like on their phones. Make them actually memorize the number so they can call from anywhere.

- **If you have to exchange children for visitations, ask a third party to do the exchange, or meet with your ex in the parking lot of a police station.** Making the meeting place public (or, even better, at a police station) will help ensure your ex doesn't become abusive with you or the children. Some police stations even have a designated spot just for this kind of transfer.

- **Make sure the school has all legal instructions and paperwork.** If you have a protective order that covers your children, provide a copy to the school along with instructions on what to do if your ex shows up wanting to see or take the children. If you don't have a protective order, give them a copy of any custody orders. If there's nothing in place and you fear for your children's safety, simply give the school instructions to call the police first and then you if anyone else tries to pick up the children.

Other safety ideas include letting your work, kids' school, neighbors, and extended family members know what is going on. You don't have to tell everyone the whole story. I'd suggest coming up with a short but sweet (and honest) explanation that you can recite when you don't want to give all the details. Here is an example:

> My husband and I are separated because of domestic violence. I have safety concerns, and I would appreciate it if you would _____ (fill in the blank: screen any calls coming in for me; make a note on my account that no one but myself is allowed access; call the police if you see anything suspicious; etc.).

The Emotional Rollercoaster Ride

Now that you're out of a relationship you worked so hard to escape, you'd think you'd feel only relief and excitement for the future. There probably are periods where you do feel those things. But, at other times, you might also feel fear and guilt about leaving; you might feel lonely and miss the good times the two of you had.

Being on an *emotional rollercoaster* is the norm after leaving your abuser. When you're with him, you're constantly in fight-or-flight mode, your primary emotion is usually fear, or you're simply numb. Once you are finally away, you'll usually feel at least some level of relief (often a *great* sense of relief). Then, just about the time you've really started to relax—just when it's really starting to sink in that you never have to go back to him—the impact of what you suffered in the relationship will set in. You no longer have to focus on him and stuff down every tear, hide every sign of frustration, bite back every angry retort.

Now It's "Me Time"

All those feelings you kept bottled up for so long bubble up to the surface. If you charted your emotions like the stock market, it'd look like a wild ride of buying and selling as the line jags up, then down, and then back up again. You might even begin to question your own sanity when one moment you're fine and going about your day, and the next you're lying on the floor crying hysterically, or feeling so angry you could rip trees out of the ground. You start to remember things he did, things that were so painful and degrading, you don't know how you even forgot about them in the first place.

These emotions seem to come out of nowhere and don't necessarily have an obvious trigger (or you're triggered by something seemingly minor). Just realize that the emotional rollercoaster is normal, and *it will pass*. Give yourself permission to be inconsistent emotionally—happy, sad, excited, lonely, angry, remorseful, regretful—in the aftermath of the breakup. All these emotions and more will likely play out inside you as you come to grips with not only the true nature of the relationship when it happened, but what being an individual—apart from him, apart from the relationship—will mean for you in the future. Engaging with these emotions and working through them mean you're already on the road to healthier self-awareness and emotional well-being—even if that road has a few potholes along the way.

> Give yourself permission to be emotionally inconsistent in the aftermath of the breakup. Engaging with these emotions and working through them mean you're already on the road to emotional wellbeing.

The Dangers of Second-Guessing—and Why You Do It

At some point, you might find yourself wondering if you made the right decision to leave in the first place:

- Did you overreact? He said he was sorry.

- Were you being too emotional? Maybe you just need to give him another chance.

- He's seen that you *will* leave. Maybe he'll take that to heart and totally change his ways.

Listen to your instincts. What if you ran into him tonight at a convenience store? What would you feel? Happy to see him—or terrified? Are you afraid to listen to the constant voicemails he's leaving you? If even the very notion of running into him fills you with fear, then you have your answer, whatever your second-guessing might try to persuade you of otherwise. If you find yourself thinking about the good times, imagine what would happen if an argument arose. How safe would you feel? How heard?

The Effects of Abuse Don't End When You Leave

Survivors of abuse almost always experience some level of residual trauma. Ironically, those effects don't always show themselves while in the relationship.

In time, you won't jump every time you see someone in the store who, for a second, you thought was your ex. You won't tense up every time you see a vehicle drive by, just like the one he drove. And don't beat yourself up with rational thoughts of "he's not even in town anymore" or "he wrecked that truck, so of course that's not him" or "I'm being stupid, weak, paranoid," or whatever other negative term you probably learned from him.

Grappling with these emotions is just part of the healing process. Be compassionate and patient with yourself. You've been through a lot. The best way to get through it more quickly is simply to take care of yourself. Practicing self-care—the item usually at the bottom of your to-do list, right?—is the best thing you can do to enable yourself to move forward faster to a brighter future. Until you take care of yourself, you can't properly take care of others, like your children, during this difficult transition period.

Survivors of abuse almost always experience some level of residual trauma. Practicing self-care will help you move forward faster to a brighter future and enable you to take care of others, like your children, during this difficult transition period.

I'm Not the Same Person I Used to Be

Being in an abusive relationship can make you question who you are, or who you used to be. Sam was a chemistry major in her junior year of college. She was petite and athletic, highly intelligent, and articulate. She'd recently broken up with her boyfriend, Shaun, whom she'd dated for three years. It became clear fairly early on that she was very self-conscious about her appearance, her performance in school, her social interactions, and every other aspect of her life. The reason for her discomfort became more apparent as stories of her relationship with Shaun unfolded:

He was very particular about how he liked his coffee, so I paid attention to every detail and would make it for him all the time. Then, one day, Shaun told me I was doing it wrong. He went on and on about how he never asks for anything big, just the small stuff, and how I can't even respect him enough to listen to him. But I'd made it just the way he showed me! I was so confused!

Everything was a lesson with him. I would be all excited about a project I was working on and show it to him, and he would start asking questions. But if I couldn't fully explain how everything worked, he would tell me how I needed to know these things if I was going to succeed. I started feeling dumb and self-conscious and questioning myself all the time.

It's Still All about Control: How He's Trained You to Think Poorly of Yourself

I've seen so many women like Sam—obviously intelligent and capable, once stubbornly independent, who have become so uncertain of themselves. The simplest decisions can seem overwhelming after a relationship with a man who questions every decision she makes. These women have either not been allowed an opinion of their own or, if they did offer one, were so often criticized and ridiculed for it that they grew scared to speak their minds. This continues after the relationship is over—not only because they expect retaliation from others but because they honestly do not know what's true or false—right or wrong—anymore. They've lived so long in an irrational mirror world—a reflection of reality created by their abuser—that they're unsure if others will think their ideas are stupid or judge them for making a "wrong" decision. Even after leaving such a relationship, the training (some would say brainwashing) by their abuser remains. They continue to torment themselves, scrutinizing everything they say or do, just as he taught them to do when he was still with them. In a way he still is with them—in their heads.

Shrug Off the Skin He Dressed You In: Find Yourself Again

Regaining your old self is a slow process and is probably more aptly described as "establishing your new self." Give yourself some room to recover. If you were in an abusive, controlling relationship for years, there's no way you can switch off the person you became in that relationship and switch on "your old self." For one thing, you're at a different place in life. You may have been a young, single twenty-something and now you're in your forties with kids. Even if you haven't been in the relationship for long, a lot has changed for you.

Figuring out who you are without him is going to be like setting out on a trip with only a vague map to guide you. As scary as that might sound, it can also be an exciting adventure. It'll be a struggle, and it'll take time. You may have to rebuild your support system and establish new (healthier for you) friendships, overcome the fears and self-doubt he created in you, or dig yourself out of a financial hole. Whatever the obstacles you face, keep one thing in mind: from now on, *you* make all the decisions. You can have lunch with a coworker without needing to get his permission or worrying about an argument ensuing later when he finds out. You can choose what to wear and whether you want to spend money getting your nails done. You can choose who comes into your home and how they treat you. There may be some quiet, lonely nights ahead, but there will also be a feeling of peace—an atmosphere no longer permeated by anger and fear—and a future full of possibilities that *you* make into realities.

> Discovering who you are is as much about rejecting the person he brainwashed you into believing you were as it is about discovering the person you can truly be: your own best friend.

One Day at a Time, One Step at a Time

Although the world is full of suffering, it is full also of the overcoming of it. — Helen Keller

Recovery and healing are a long road. For now, take joy in the small things. If you can go buy groceries by yourself without worrying about whether a man is looking at you, appreciate that sense of freedom. If you can walk into your home without a tightness in your chest because you're worried what someone's emotional state is, enjoy the feeling of walking into your own home *relaxed*—which is how it should be!

Make a list of all the things that are different in your life, now that you're out of the relationship. One of my clients made a list of reasons to stay single in order to help herself through the evenings when she felt lonely. She titled it "101 Reasons" but found herself struggling to reach 101. In the process of trying to achieve that number, she began paying more attention to her life as a single mother. She recognized not just how things had changed, but how much stronger she now saw herself as a person. Below are about half the items from her list. Some of them are tongue-in-cheek, but all of them are absolutely true to her experience.

Reasons to Stay Single

1. I am a whole person. I do not need someone else to make me whole.
2. No "lessons" on the proper way to load the dishwasher, sort the clothes, clean the kitchen, etc.
3. No sexist views/remarks about men and women's roles, jobs, etc.
4. Peace and quiet.
5. No arguing, guilt trips, or silent treatment.
6. Fewer "parenting issues" my son will have to work through in therapy as an adult.
7. Antidepressants are expensive.
8. Therapy is expensive.
9. Xanax is addictive.
10. Filing protective orders can be so time-consuming.
11. I'd rather bitch to girlfriends over a glass of wine than write it all down in an annulment.
12. I can choose my own décor.
13. Divorce lawyers are expensive.
14. Romantic comedies don't get ruined at the best part.
15. Drive where you want, when you want, and how you want without unsolicited directions (or criticism).
16. No more holidays or vacations with the in-laws where my return trip mantra is "I'll never do this again."
17. Less testosterone in the car equals less road rage on the street.
18. My tongue is much less sore from not having to bite it all the time.
19. No need to ask permission for anything I do.
20. No jealousy or unfounded accusations.
21. I will never again live with a packed bag in the trunk of my car, ready to flee at a moment's notice.

22. Clean the house or leave it messy; it all depends on my mood.

23. Complete control of the remote and what I watch.

24. If someone's being an ass, I ditch them—not drive home with them.

25. Choose my own friends without anyone else's input or opinion.

26. I've become more financially stable with one income than we ever were with two.

27. It's so much easier to learn to like yourself when there's not someone pointing out all your supposed flaws every day.

28. No one else to take credit for my accomplishments or blame me for their failures.

29. To shave or not to shave ... who gives a damn?

30. In fairy tales, you kiss the frog and get a prince. In real life, sometimes you kiss the prince but get a frog.

31. No snide comments or sarcastic barbs—other than mine.

32. Being stalked gets old so quickly.

33. If I want drama, I'll go to a play.

34. If I lack companionship, I'll adopt a dog.

35. Go to bed at whatever time I want.

36. Never feel smothered.

37. Opportunity to explore my own interests, ideas, and opinions without judgment.

38. My well of patience is no longer as dry as the Sahara (which is good for my son).

39. No flying coffee cups or other dishes.

40. More room for my clothes in the closet (which is a great excuse to get more clothes).

41. No getting embarrassed over the other person's public comments or behavior.

42. No investing large amounts of time in activities that don't interest me.

43. No one else has veto power over my decisions.

44. All of a sudden, everything isn't my fault.

45. "Living in fear" is an oxymoron. You're not really living.

46. No invasions of privacy.

47. Life has taken on a refreshing level of simplicity.

48. I find myself much less worried about the type of man my son will grow up to be.

49. If anyone in this house throws a fit, I'll just ground him.

50. As exciting as it was to get my first subpoena, it's one of those experiences that really doesn't need repeating.

51. Watching *Gaslight* shouldn't make me think of my marriage.

52. I've reached my maximum lifetime capacity for interactions with narcissists.

53. No need to prove my level of commitment to anyone other than myself.

54. There's just something inherently wrong when you see a cop walking down your street with a rifle and your first thought is "Oh, good. He's not stopping here."

Consider writing your own list. Your list may be titled "Reasons I Have to Admire Myself" or "Reasons I Deserve Love and Respect" or "Obstacles I Have Overcome." Whatever your list's title, push yourself to expand on its length. Put it in a place where you will see it every day to remind yourself just how far you've come. Become your own biggest supporter and cheerleader, and surround yourself with others who support you too.

Seeking Support from Others

I would like to say that everyone in your life will be supportive, but that's not likely. It's just not realistic—and I want to keep your expectations realistic. Some people will have an easy time accepting that what the abuser is doing isn't fair or normal or healthy, but still don't think you should leave or divorce him. Maybe they believe in the myths about what is abuse and why it happens. They may feel that you just need to go to couples counseling or that he just needs to get sober or get on medication and everything will be okay.

Jane came from a close-knit, very religious family. She describes their reaction to her unhappiness in her marriage to Rob:

> We'd been married for 16 years and had three kids. I used to make excuses for him. It was always "when this happens, things will get better," but we'd reach those milestones, and I'd have to make another excuse.
>
> I finally started to open up to my family about what we were dealing with. They were supportive but kept saying things like "every marriage goes through this" and "you owe it to your kids to work this out." There are unspoken rules in my family like "God hates divorce."
>
> The first time I left him, I stayed with my parents. Of course, he started acting like the man I fell in love with. He was repentant and said he just wanted his family back. I was skeptical; I'd heard the promises before. But my parents would invite him over for Sunday dinner, without even asking me! I was still so angry at him, but he was being so polite and attentive to the children and me … I worried I'd look like the horrible one if I wasn't polite and accepting in return. Between his pleading and promises and my family's pressure to work things out, I gave in and went back. Things were good—for a few months—but of course, we ended up right back at the same place.

This might be hard to hear, but if your friends and family are urging you to do something you don't want to do—that your instincts tell you is not only not right but potentially dangerous—like going back to your abuser, *don't listen to them.* Find support elsewhere (e.g., other friends who are more understanding or a counselor). You don't need judgment from others right now; you need unconditional support and understanding.

A Word Regarding Friends and Family

The person that your family and friends see and interact with is often a man on his best behavior. He's kind and polite and seems to be a wonderful husband and father. It can be very hard for people to accept the fact that someone they thought they knew is not actually a decent, caring family man. It's like finding out that a favorite teacher or childhood hero has been arrested for a horrible crime—it just doesn't fit with the image of the person you created in your mind. This can be tough for most people to process right away. As humans, we don't like to accept the fact that we can be so easily deceived or that we can't tell the good guys from the bad just by looking at them.

One of my reasons for writing this guide is to educate family and friends who truly want to be supportive. But because they have no experience with domestic violence or how it impacts victims—what causes it and what can happen—they may inadvertently give bad advice or make you feel guilty for wanting to leave the relationship. I am hopeful that educating themselves a bit on the topic will help them be better able to support you. So please—if you feel comfortable with a loved one or friend—share this guide with them so they can get a better idea of what you're going through.

> Rely on friends and family for support when you can, but they should be kind and understanding, not judgmental or unsympathetic. And seek help from an unbiased, mental-health professional if possible.

Even if you have a good support system, I can't recommend highly enough that you reach out to a DV agency, whether that's a local shelter or a national hotline. Having someone knowledgeable about domestic violence to talk to and who can offer support and advice is invaluable to keeping you safe and helping the healing process. You're the expert on your situation and your partner's behavior, but they can help you make decisions from a place of rational thought, not emotionality. That's something family and friends may not be able to do because they love you (and might react emotionally to your situation). In addition, it can just be really nice to talk to someone that gets it, without the need for long explanations and examples that cause you pain to repeat.

If you're a family member or friend of someone experiencing domestic violence, please see the "For Family and Friends" section.

What's Going to Happen to My Children?

> *If there must be trouble, let it be in my day,*
> *that my child may have peace.* — *Thomas Paine*

Post-Separation Power and Control Wheel

I'd like to be able to tell you that a man who's been charged with family violence will automatically have his visitation rights to his children restricted (or taken away altogether). Unfortunately, some courts don't seem to understand the impact of domestic violence on children when they're not physically involved (i.e., when they simply witness their mother being abused). This means that the abuser will often have contact with the children during a separation and can use them as a way of hurting you. The Post-Separation Power and Control Wheel offers good examples of how he might use your own children against you.

© COPYRIGHT 2013 DOMESTIC
ABUSE INTERVENTION PROGRAMS
202 East Superior Street
Duluth, MN 55802
218-722-2781
www.theduluthmodel.org

Even if visitation is restricted, the children will likely experience a lasting emotional impact of having witnessed degradation and control being modeled and violence inflicted.

Children's Reactions

Children can have a wide variety of possible reactions to their parents separating. Some kids will be excited and relieved that you're finally leaving the father (or stepfather) they've come to detest. Other kids will be upset and just want things to go back to "normal," even if their version of normal hasn't been very healthy for them. Some kids will even choose to stay with the abuser if given a chance. It's not uncommon for a child to side with the seemingly stronger, more powerful parent because they feel safer there. Or maybe that parent can afford to buy them nicer gifts or has fewer house rules or simply guilts the child into "not abandoning them."

Even if the kids are happy to go with you and seem relieved to leave the abusive situation, they may have emotional difficulties in the future. Their life is going to be disrupted, not only because one of their parents is gone, but because they may have to leave their home, live with family members or in a shelter, change schools, or make other difficult transitions—on top of dealing with the domestic violence.

As they wrestle with the fallout of leaving a DV situation, kids will often go to one extreme or another behaviorally. Some will try to be the "perfect kid" and do everything right in a desperate attempt to keep everyone around them happy (as a way of keeping themselves safe). Other kids will act out, getting into trouble at school and becoming involved in fights. Sometimes you won't even see behavioral problems until weeks after the separation, when it finally sinks in for the children that they really are in a safe place (and can, therefore, exhibit a range of emotions without fear of losing another parent). Just as with adult victims, the emotions they've been struggling with will eventually bubble to the surface. Unfortunately, the safe parent—the one they know will never leave them—is often the target of their anger and pain; they can safely be a monster and still trust they will be loved and protected. It's somewhat ironic but often true.

The Helping Your Kids through the Separation Checklist

So, what can you do to help your kids get through the separation? This list will give you some ideas, though it's not exhaustive by any means. Every child is unique. Talking with a DV counselor can help you find the best way to support your kids and their individual needs.

- **Take care of yourself.** You're like a pitcher of water. You may tend to try to give of yourself to everyone else. But if you don't take the time to refill that pitcher, you'll have nothing left to give anyone else—not even your kids.

- **Realize that every kid is different.** You may have one kid that's thrilled with the new arrangements, another that's worried and trying to take care of you, and a third that misses Dad and is acting out every two minutes. Respect the fact that each child is going to have his or her own unique set of feelings and expresses them differently. That means each needs to be handled differently. *Listen to them.* They can tell you, better than anyone else, what they're struggling with and what they need from you.

- **Understand that you can't shield them from all pain and suffering.** As tempting as it is to try and shield your children from everything as a parent, that's not your job. It's not even in your child's best interests to have a pain-free life. Don't give in to the temptation to relax rules or spoil them to make up for what they're going through. They need structure in their life—including a parent they can rely on to be consistent in their discipline—now more than ever.

- **Be a safe person for them to talk to.** It needs to be okay for your kids to talk to you about what they're feeling, including missing their father or being angry at him. It's also okay for them to see you upset sometimes. Be honest with them, but talk to them at their age level.

- **Don't make them *your* confidante.** It's okay to tell them basic information for safety reasons or explain that you can't buy them something because money is tight or let them know that since you have to work more, you need their help around the house. What your kids *don't* need to know is everything their father did (or is still doing) to abuse you or how far behind he is on child support or how lonely and overwhelmed you're feeling. Those are issues that you need to share with another adult (and great things to share with a counselor or other mental-health professional).

- **Review the Children's Bill of Rights in Appendix B of this guide**. You can't enforce these rights in their father's home, but you can in yours and can make your kids familiar with them. A child who feels valued will recover from the emotional trauma more quickly than a child who doesn't.

- **Make your home a safe haven.** You can't control what goes on in their father's house, but even if he has primary custody, you can provide your kids with a shelter in the storm. Make your home an example of what a stable and healthy life should look like. This can have a greater impact than you can possibly imagine.

- **Seek professional help if you feel it's needed.** Not every kid will need to see a counselor, but it never hurts to provide them their own professional to talk to. This is especially true if the problems between you and your ex become long and drawn out, he's using the kids as weapons against you, or your kids continue to have problems after the turbulence of the transition period has settled down.

Orders of Protection

Should I Get a Restraining Order?

Every state is different in terminology and specifics regarding orders of protection. (For example, some states call orders of protection "protective orders," and some call them "restraining orders.") The following is a very general overview about orders of protection. I recommend going to https://www.womenslaw.org/ to get information about the state you currently reside in.

Protective order statutes give courts the right to order your abuser to stop hurting or threatening you. Most states also include orders to stay away from you, your home, your job, and/or your school. You can also ask the court to order "no contact" (to include phone calls, texts, contacts through a third person, etc.).

Depending on the state and the particular statutes it works under, the court may order the abuser to pay child support, make house payments, make decisions about custody and visitation of your children, etc. All of these provisions will be in place temporarily, awaiting final decisions that will be made later, perhaps as the result of divorce proceedings. Other possible court orders include requiring the abuser to turn over any firearms, attend a treatment program, etc.

If the abuser fails to comply with the court order, you can ask the police or the court (or both) to enforce the order. The police will usually enforce orders that need an immediate response, such as a no-contact order or an order requiring the abuser to leave the home you both own. Depending on the violation, the abuser could face misdemeanor or felony criminal charges.

I live in Texas, so I'm able to provide more detail about securing an order of protection in Texas. You may live in another state that has a similar process, in which case the next section may prove helpful. However, you cannot count on any two states being exactly alike. Look to the resources listed in this section to learn how your state handles orders of protection.

The Restraining Order in Texas

In Texas, a *civil restraining order* is a legal document that a lawyer writes up. If the order is granted, the abuser is required to stay away from you, your property, etc. However, if he violates the civil restraining order and you call the police, *he won't necessarily get arrested.* You can take him back to court and show that he has violated the order, but when he's actually standing on your doorstep, the police are probably going to ask him to leave, not arrest him. Violating a civil restraining order will likely only result in a judge (at worst) finding your ex in contempt of court, which might earn him a few days in jail and a fine.

Still, in less physically volatile cases—or cases where the victim is unable to obtain a protective order (discussed next)—a civil restraining order can be a helpful alternative. Some individuals simply ask that it be included with initial divorce documentation that each person stays away from the other and their respective property. Again, *this is a civil matter* and not one that police are likely to enforce, other than to ask your ex to leave if he is on your property or at your place of business.

The Protective Order in Texas

A *protective order* is also assigned by a civil court, but violation can lead to immediate arrest because, in Texas, violating a protective order is a Class A misdemeanor (Texas Penal Code § 25.071) or a third-degree felony if the perpetrator is convicted of violating it three times. A protective order requires one person to cease harassing or abusing (whether in person or through technology, such as cell phones and social media) another person for a specified period of time.

Protective orders are usually approved when physical violence or a threat of physical violence has occurred, and they will go on an individual's criminal record. The protective order requires that the abuser stay away from the victim's home and work and may also require the abuser to stay away from the victim's children. On top of that, the abuser may make no attempt to contact the victim or her family in any way. This means the abuser is not allowed to call you, write to you, send messages through friends or family, make comments on your social media, or make contact in any other way.

To file for a protective order, a victim can go through a lawyer or can simply fill out the paperwork herself at the county attorney's office. When a protective order is first provided, it's almost always a *temporary order*, usually good for about two weeks. A date will be set for a formal hearing in which you can request a permanent order, which, if granted, is usually good for up to two years (despite its name). The abuser will be served papers regarding the order, and he has the right to be at the hearing. (Feel free to ask for a security escort, bring a friend, or contact a DV advocate to accompany you. You don't need to face him alone!) The judge can make basic decisions about who gets to live in the house, whether there will be visitation with the children, and other subjects of mutual interest. If you don't show up for the hearing, the temporary protective order will simply expire, and nothing more will be done. After it expires, you will have no legal protection to help protect you from your abuser.

Resources: Protective Orders

Different states handle orders of protection differently. They even call them different things. Research how your particular state deals with orders of protection.

http://www.womenslaw.org

http://family.findlaw.com/domestic-violence/domestic-violence-orders-of-protection-and-restraining-orders.html

---

Who's Legally Obligated by the Order?

One thing about a protective order—it's your **abuser's** order. If, a few weeks after you leave, you feel lonely and nostalgic and reach out to him, *you* have not violated the protective order. If you've gotten used to letting him come around and see the kids, but now he's starting to get possessive and controlling again and you want to cut contact, *you have that right.* The protective order is still in place, and you have every right to enforce it any time you want.

Whether you invite him over or not, he's the one in trouble with the justice system. It's *his* responsibility not to violate the restrictions that he has earned for himself, just as someone who is on probation often loses the right to drink, even if that's not what they were arrested for.

Keep in Mind, It's Just a Piece of Paper

I vividly remember the day I watched a judge sign a protective order for a woman and, before handing it to her, waved it in front on her with the warning, "Remember, this can't stop a bullet." At the end of the day, a protective order is just a piece of paper—not a physical shield—so while it can help hold your abuser accountable, you still need to take your own precautions to stay safe.

In fact, just like being served divorce papers, being served a protective order may trigger an abuser to act out. That doesn't automatically mean you shouldn't get one. Like a divorce, it's about what's most important in the long term. Just in case, take extra precautions for at least the first few days after any papers are served, or after any other event you think might trigger your ex. Continue the safety plan (e.g., avoiding communication) you adopted when you left. As suggested earlier, make your employer aware of the situation (e.g., ask them to screen calls and prohibit your ex from coming into your work location).

> At the end of the day, a protective order is just a piece of paper—not a physical shield. It can help hold your abuser accountable, but you still need to take your own precautions to stay safe.

Documentation Is Key in Court

If you have a protective order and he violates it, make a police report—every time. Even if it's just that he sent you a letter or called you. *Document everything.* Even if you don't have a protective order, *document everything.* Simply noting the date, time, and a brief description of what happened can help build a harassment case should you need to do so later. As much as you might want to, don't delete texts, emails, or social media posts without getting a screenshot or saving them on a computer. If reading or listening to them makes you upset, ask someone you trust to do this for you.

Basically, assume that you are going to have a stalker whose sole purpose in life is to make *your* life more difficult. As frustrating and mentally exhausting as this can be, *remember*: he used to torment you daily, and you had no escape—then. *Now*, you have hope for a better life. Don't surrender your newfound power to him again; keep the boundaries you set when you escaped. You no longer have to simply suck it up and appease him.

What If You Have a Protective Order in One State but Move to Another?

In 2013, the U.S. Department of Justice reauthorized the Violence against Women Act, which states that protection orders from one state are entitled to "full faith and credit" in any other state. In short, no matter where you secure an order of protection in the United States, its protections apply to you in all 50 states.

For example, let's say you have a protective order from Maine barring your abuser from contact with you, your family members, or your children; then you move to Texas to start over. You move in with relatives and enroll your kids in school. A week later, you walk out the door and your ex is parked on the street out front. He's demanding to know where the kids are, saying that he has a right to see them and just wants to take them lunch at school. If you call the police, they are obligated to enforce your protective order (*which you should always have a copy of on hand*), just as if it were given out by a Texas judge.

If you do move—including within state—be sure to contact the court that originally granted your protective order and give the clerk your new address so your new residence will be a protected location under the original order.

For more information on getting a protective order in Texas, check out Texas Law Help: https://texaslawhelp.org/toolkit/i-need-protective-order.

The Things to Know about Protective Orders Checklist

- **It's different from a civil restraining order**. Only a protective order is a violation of the Texas penal code and, therefore, enforceable by the police. If you move to another state (like California), be aware they might call their protective orders restraining orders. If unsure, ask if the order you're seeking is enforced by the penal code of the state you're in.

- **It prohibits the abuser from harassing you in any way, not just physically**. Texts, phone calls, emails—the form of contact doesn't matter. It's the contact itself that constitutes a violation of the order.

- **It can apply to your children as well as you (depending on how the order is written)**. If covered by the order, your children enjoy the exact same protections as you do.

- **You can apply for a protective order without engaging a lawyer**. While legal help can facilitate securing an order, if you can't afford a lawyer, you can still secure a protective order by filling out the paperwork yourself at your county attorney's office.

- **It applies to the abuser, not you**. If, for example, you choose to allow the abuser to visit the children at your apartment, *you* are not violating the order.

- **Document everything when an abuser violates the order**. Save texts, phone messages, threatening notes—any time he contacts you after the order is put in place is a violation of the order and is important evidence should he be arrested.

- **It's enforceable, no matter what state you live in.** You might have secured the order in State A, but State B is required to enforce it by U.S. law.

For Family and Friends

*The only thing necessary for the triumph of evil
is that good men should do nothing.* — *Edmund Burke*

I highly recommend that anyone who has a loved one who is, or was, in an abusive relationship read this entire guide to gain a better understanding of what she's endured. It's likely her struggle isn't over, even if the abuser is no longer in her life. This section offers suggestions of how you can help by becoming part of her support system.

The number-one thing you can do? Avoid judgment! Even if you might have experienced domestic violence yourself, you don't know what her *specific* experience is. If you believe in the sanctity of marriage—that God put two people together—that's great. But guilting her into going back because "divorce is a sin" could get her or her kids killed. If you can't be supportive in a way that encourages her to leave a bad relationship, it's better to simply tell her "I can't be there for you in this case."

Your Love and Support Are Crucial to Her Healing

It is so much more difficult for a woman to leave an abusive partner when she doesn't have a support system. Very often, it's the small things you say and do that have the greatest long-term impact. If you've become frustrated or discouraged because you've wanted your loved one to get out of an abusive relationship for a long time and she persists in staying, don't give up!

As tempting as it might be to pull her aside and scream at her to "leave him already!" don't do it. She has to make that decision on her own, when she's ready. She's already got someone in her life whom she believes loves her but is overbearing and demanding. The last thing she needs is for others in her life—no matter how well intentioned—to tell her what she should do. Also—if the abuser finds out you've counseled her to leave him, it provides him the perfect excuse to isolate her from you, telling her that you're rude to him, obviously don't like him, or are trying to break them up. You could become a reason he abuses her, making her life miserable any time she talks to you. She might even break off communication with you to avoid an argument with him. Remember: her reaching for freedom has to come in her own time, not on your timeline.

Five Tasks for Family and Friends

1. Avoid judging her.

2. Be a gatekeeper for contact with the abuser.

3. Encourage her to get professional help.

4. Foster hope for the future.

5. Be patient with her process.

It Ain't Over Till It's Over

When she does leave him, you'll probably be elated and think that it's all over. Now you can bash him and tell her what a horrible person you always knew he was and how you're so happy she's finally free of him. But what if she goes back?

You might feel betrayed—you've invested all this emotional energy in supporting her, maybe even offered her a place to stay rent-free for a while or paid expenses to help her move out, and now she goes back to him? What's she thinking?! You might even be ready to throw up your hands and say, "If this is what she really wants, I'm done helping her!"

That's a natural reaction that comes from a place of love for her. You can't stand to see her hurt, so it's easier for you to be angry with her for putting herself back in that situation. But fight that urge to lash out at her.

More often than not, a DV survivor leaves in stages—she might leave him and spend the weekend at your apartment, but on Monday she goes back. The next time she leaves, it'll be for a longer period. Eventually, it will be permanent. In particular, if she's married to her abuser or they have children together, the victim will often feel that they have a moral obligation to "give it one more try." (Other family or friends might even be pressuring her to do that.)

Also, the abuser knows her well. When times were good, he listened to all her stories. She shared her deepest secrets and greatest fears with him. He knows her inside and out, and knows exactly what buttons to push to keep her under his control, including getting her back when she leaves him. (See "What Should I Expect from Him over the Long Term?" in this guide.)

Things You Can Do to Help

So, what can you do to help her until she leaves him for good? You can validate her as a human being, working against what the abuser has done in breaking her down:

- Tell her all the things that the primary person in her life should be telling her but isn't: that you love her, for starters.
- Remind her of what a great person she is.
- Compliment her strengths.
- Listen to her, but keep the advice to a minimum unless she specifically asks for it.

It's okay to say, "I don't like it when he talks to you like that" or "I wish he would treat you better. You deserve better," but then let it go. Even if she defends him—which she probably will—don't let it devolve into an argument. Just tell her you love her and want the best for her, and change the subject to something less stressful. Plant the seed for change and encourage it to grow over time, but don't beat it into the ground. Trust me, she will hold on to your words. She will hide them away in her heart and her mind, and they might very well make a difference over time.

Latoya was one of the most memorable clients I ever worked with because of the harrowing story she told:

> He had beaten me really badly, and I was tied up, sitting on the bed. He pulled out a blanket and spread it out over the couch. I knew it was to get rid of me, that he was going to kill me. I started telling him "Baby, it's okay. I love you. We're gonna get through this." He finally cut me loose, but I couldn't leave. He wouldn't leave the apartment for two days. Finally, he went to buy cigarettes, and I snuck out and ran to my sister's place down the street.

As horrible as this experience was, it was the next part of her story that brought her to tears:

> I know I can never go back. I know he'd kill me. I have a five-year-old little girl. I have to be here for her, but I still keep thinking about him. He's in jail right now, and I wonder if he's got money on his account and if he's safe, and I hate myself for it. I hate myself that I worry about him, after what he did.

This reaction by a DV survivor, even in the worst of situations, is completely normal. Love is not a switch that can be turned off because you, intellectually, choose to stop being with someone. Realizing that a person is not healthy for you does not make you stop caring about him.

We would never demand of a prisoner of war or a kidnapping victim who's been held in captivity for a decade, "You've been out of that situation for a whole year. Why aren't you over it already?" And yet, we say that to victims months—or even weeks—after they've left their abusers.

Don't they have the right to their psychological scars, just like the POW or kidnapping victim? After all, it wasn't just an enemy who held them captive, someone they could easily fear or hate. It was the person they chose to spend the rest of their life with, the person who'd once made them feel so special and important—the person they lived with, laughed with, and loved. Often, he's the father of their children. The betrayal she suffered at the hands of the man she trusted most will take a long time to heal; the emotional scars of that mistreatment often take even longer.

The Supporting My Loved One Checklist

So, what can you do to support her and help her maintain her resolve to stay away? Here are a few suggestions:

- **Be accepting of the fact that she still loves him**. Her mind has made the decision to leave. Her heart is still unsure. Give her time to make them match.

- **Help screen calls and texts**. Offer to be the gatekeeper for her phone (texts/calls) and computer (email). Be the one to listen to the hateful, nasty messages he leaves and archive them for court later. Be the rational, thoughtful friend. She may be under so much stress that it's difficult to think clearly.

- **Be the designated supervisor of kid visits or exchanges**. If you're comfortable dealing directly with the abuser, offer to drive the kids to any court-required supervised visits. The less contact (direct or otherwise) she has with him, the less stressed (and able to make good decisions) she'll be.

- **Go with her to get her stuff**. Again, this is a comfort thing—if there's any chance he might be there (and most especially armed or otherwise threatening), ask for a police escort and go with her to pick up her things from their shared residence.

- **Encourage her to list what he would need to do to prove to her he's changed**. Relationships aren't 100 percent unsalvageable. Though most abusers don't change, some do realize their faults and can work hard to change. If she decides to give it another chance, help her make a reasonable list of "Things He Must Do to Prove He's Serious about Changing" and then help her hold him accountable to those.

- **Encourage her to get professional help**. You're a great source of support—you've proven that already. But you're probably not a trained mental-health professional. A counselor can address issues with her that you can't, but a counselor can't be a best friend—that's your job. You each have a role to play in her recovery.

- **Be understanding when she's not over it in a few weeks, months, or even years**. Emotional recovery from a traumatic experience like domestic violence takes time. If she were sick with the flu and took a week to recover instead of two days, like your brother last year, would you blame her for being weak? Emotional trauma is the same. Some women take years to recover from domestic abuse. It's her timeline, not yours.

Remember, when it comes to interacting with him or otherwise meeting him by chance, face to face: *your* safety and *her* safety always come first. Don't be brave—be safe!

A Final Word of Encouragement ... and Hope

Life can only be understood backwards;
but it must be lived forwards. — Søren Kierkegaard

Look back on your life with your abuser. That's the roadmap to the life you will have moving forward if you stay in the relationship. If you don't like where that road is leading, then it's time to take another path—one of freedom, where you get to make your own choices. It's a road where others can walk with you, healthy people who support you. It's a road where you get to determine the destination; where you're in control of your own life and where you want to go with it.

Being in an abusive relationship is very much like being held prisoner. More than that, it's like being a prisoner of war. POWs are not only held against their will—they are tortured, humiliated, and forced to submit to the will of their captors. *Anyone* that simply *survives* such an ordeal is seen as a hero, and that makes you a hero, too.

Whether you are out of your abusive situation yet or not, you're still here. You're still alive. And while you're alive, there's still hope. And you're reading this guide. By doing so, you're showing yourself and others that you want something more for your life, something better.

Very few people—other than those who've also experienced domestic violence or those who work daily to help survivors bring an end to the violence—will understand exactly what you're going through. Not everyone will recognize the courage you've shown, and continue to show, in the face of fear. Make no mistake:

- You *are* brave.
- You are *strong*.
- *You* are courageous.

You could not have made it this far if you weren't. And a better future, a life of freedom, is possible. It's not an easy journey, but it *is* one with a real future, full of possibilities. You've already taken your first step into that better future by reading this guide.

Keep going. Find help. Reclaim your life.

Reclaim yourself.

Appendix A: Resources

Books

- Why Does He Do That?: Inside the Minds of Angry and Controlling Men by Lundy Bancroft. Available on Amazon at https://a.co/d/cA5PdJr.

- Should I Stay or Should I Go?: A Guide to Knowing If Your Relationship Can—and Should—Be Saved by Lundy Bancroft and J.A.C. Patrissi. Available on Amazon at https://a.co/d/7eoX7mO.

- The Verbally Abusive Relationship: How to Recognize It and How to Respond by Patricia Evans. Available on Amazon at https://a.co/d/iVnOoTi.

- The Emotionally Destructive Marriage: How to Find Your Voice and Reclaim Your Hope by Leslie Vernick. Available on Amazon at https://a.co/d/2PRbAa9.

- *It's My Life Now: Starting Over after an Abusive Relationship or Domestic Violence* by Meg Kennedy Dugan and Roger R. Hock. Available on Amazon at https://a.co/d/4QAKMbS.

- *Boundaries in Marriage* by Henry Cloud and John Townsend. Available on Amazon at https://a.co/d/5MeeBVY.

- *Crazy Love* by Leslie Morgan Steiner. Available on Amazon at https://a.co/d/dUZtnZ8.

- *Not to People Like Us: Hidden Abuse in Upscale Marriages* by Susan Weitzman. Available on Amazon at https://a.co/d/hG41vVi.

- *Is It My Fault?: Hope and Healing for Those Suffering Domestic Violence* by Lindsey A. Holcomb and Justin S. Holcomb. Available on Amazon at https://a.co/d/2qaDcw1.

Websites

- Power and Control Wheels: https://www.theduluth-model.org/wheels/

- Nation Coalition against Domestic Violence: http://www.ncadv.org/

- The National Domestic Violence Hotline: www.thehotline.org

- The Childhood Domestic Violence Association: https://cdv.org/

- Battered Women's Justice Project: http://www.bwjp.org/

- Mosaic Threat Assessment Systems: https://www.mosaic-method.com/

- Stalking Prevention, Awareness, & Resource Center (SPARC): https://www.stalkingawareness.org

- Animal Welfare Institute Safe Havens: https://awionline.org/safe-havens

Safety Planning

- Domestic Violence Personalized Safety Plan. http://www.ncdsv.org/images/DV_Safety_Plan.pdf

- Safety Planning. https://www.dvrc-or.org/safety-planning/
- What Is a Safety Plan? http://www.thehotline.org/help/path-to-safety/
- A Sample Safety Planning Tool. http://lcadv.org/wp-content/uploads/2012/04/Safety_Plan.pdf

Information about Orders of Protection

- WomensLaw.org: www.womenslaw.org
- Texas Law Help: https://texaslawhelp.org/toolkit/i-need-protective-order
- Domestic Violence: Orders of Protection and Restraining Orders: http://family.findlaw.com/domestic-violence/domestic-violence-orders-of-protection-and-restraining-orders.html

Appendix B: Divorced Children's Bill of Rights

There are a number of different versions of the Divorced Children's Bill of Rights. A few are listed below. All of them place the welfare, interests, and emotional, mental, and physical well-being of children first and foremost. Here are a handful of the principles embraced by most of these statements of rights.

- The right not to be asked or expected to choose sides or be put in a situation where I would
- The right to be treated as a person and not as a pawn, possession or negotiating chip.
- The right to freely and privately communicate with both parents.
- The right not to be asked questions by one parent about the other.

I also recommend the article "What Parents Can Do to Help Children with Divorce" by Kathleen O'Connell Corcoran and available at https://www.mediate.com/articles/koc.cfm. The article goes into more detail about how parents can minimize the impacts of divorce on children. For other examples of the Divorced Children's Bill of Rights, see the selected list below.

Website Resources

- Emery, Robert E. *Psychology Today*. Children's Bill of Rights in Divorce. https://www.psychology-today.com/us/blog/divorced-children/201009/childrens-bill-rights-in-divorce.

- Mathur, Rricha. Children's Bill of Rights. https://campaignforchildren.org/resources/fact-sheet/childrens-bill-of-rights/.

- Robertson, Rob V. Children's Rights. https://www.travis-countytx.gov/dro/children-rights.

- General divorce information: https://www.divorcenet.com/.

About the Author

Alison Pourteau holds a master's degree in clinical psychology and a bachelor's degree in psychology, both from Sam Houston State University. She is a Licensed Professional Counselor–Supervisor (LPC-S) in the state of Texas and mentors and oversees clinical hours for new counselor interns seeking post-graduate licensure.

She has served as the chairperson of the Brazos County Coalition Against Domestic Violence and was a founding member of the 501(c)3 non-profit Brazos Valley Counseling Services, which provided affordable counseling services to low- and middle-income families and children. She has provided counseling services to Twin City Domestic Violence Services clientele and has overseen counselors and counseling program for the Sexual Assault Resource Center of the Brazos Valley. She served as an adjunct professor at Blinn College, teaching general psychology and lifespan development. Currently, she works as the Director of Clinical Services at Scotty's House Child Advocacy Center in Bryan, Texas, and Alison testifies as an expert in cases of family violence, child abuse, and adult sexual assault. She also maintains a private practice. Alison has been the recipient of the Robert E. "Bob" Wiatt Lifetime Achievement Award (2014) and the Margaret Lalk Victim Advocacy Award (2024) for her work with trauma survivors.

If you'd like to let her know what you think about this guide, please email her at reclaimyourlifeyourself@gmail.com. Alison lives in College Station, Texas, with her family.

Your Thoughts / Notes

I would encourage you to use this space to write down thoughts, ideas, memories—things that you want to come back to. If you're trying to decide if your relationship is abusive, this can be a place to brainstorm (though I strongly recommend you keep the book well hidden).

If you're out of the relationship, this book may trigger memories of things you went through; maybe things you didn't even recognize as abuse at the time. Take a minute to journal about them. Or, write out some plans and goals for your future. Start your own "101 Reasons" list of why your life is better now, or how it will be better in the future.

If you're reading this book because a loved one is in an abusive relationship, jot down thoughts you want to share with them, or just write out "I can't make them leave. They have to make the decision on their own, when they are ready" 100 times until you feel like it's starting to sink in, even if you find it difficult to accept.

This is your space. Use it as you need. Make it your own.

_____

_____

_____

_____

_____

_____

_____